The written works of Graeme Edge

Excerpts with kind permission of EMI Publishing and Westminster Publishing

Book design by David Byrd

Compiled and edited by Gordon 'Gordy' Marshall

The Written Works of Graeme Edge

1967 – **Days of Future Passed:-** Morning Glory - Late Lament

1968 – **In Search of The Lost Chord:** - Departure – The Word

1969 – **On the Threshold of a Dream:** - In the Beginning – The Dream

1969 – **To Our Children's Children's Children:** - Higher & Higher

1970 – **A Question of Balance:** - The Balance

1971 – **Every Good Boy Deserves Favour:** - After You Came

1972 – **Seventh Sojourn:** - You and Me

1978 – **Octave:** - I'll Be Level With You

1981 – **Long Distance Voyager:** - 22,000 Days

1983 – **The Present:** - Going Nowhere

1986 – **The Other Side Of Life:** - The Spirit

1999 – **Strange Times:** - Nothing Changes

SOLO   (The Graeme Edge Band)

1974 –   **Kick Off Your Muddy Boots:** - Lost in Spaces - Shotgun - Something We'd Like to Say - In Dreams - Have You Ever Wondered

1977 –   **Paradise Ballroom:** - Paradise Ballroom - Human - Down, Down, Down - In the Night of the Light - Be My Eyes

Foreword

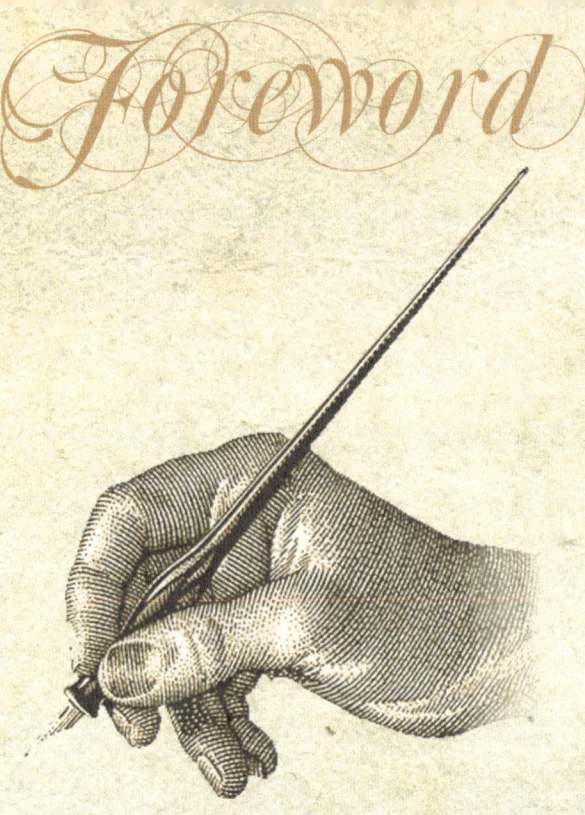

*I*s it the ingenuity in the technique, or the scale of the creativity? Both things are necessary for a poet, yet they fall behind the most essential element – the ability to evoke emotion. Good poets and lyricists have an additional intrinsic sense that tells them what others would like to hear at a particular time. The result is often a work of art that stays in the memory of the person who reads the prose or listens to the music.

Our individual histories are strung together with words and music – relating the lyrics and melodies to the people who were with us, at the place or event where we first encountered them. Just like a time machine, they have the ability to transport us through the years to recapture the love, heartbreak, joy, grief, success, failure and myriad other emotions experienced throughout our lives, reinforcing the memories that make us who we are, and help (if only a little bit) make sense of the world.

You are holding in your hands the poetic works of Graeme Edge, the drummer and one of the founding members of the legendary rock band, The Moody Blues. This is the first time Graeme's written works have been collated into one published document.

I have been working closely with this remarkable bard and musician for over twenty years, but the decision to put his written material into one place only came about recently... actually while eating Dungeness crab at a waterfront restaurant in Seattle, during a recent Moody Blues tour of the United States.

We were oscillating betwixt several topics over dinner that evening, including some heavy political debate, various amusing touring anecdotes and Graeme's poetry. The result of the evening's discussions ended with the decision to complete this book.

After dinner we left the restaurant and continued our evening together leaning against the railings on the pier. In the warm summer evening, watching ferries sailing back and forth across Seattle Harbour, we discussed how the book might look.

As well as being a voluminous reader, Graeme has written poetry his entire life, and if I'm not mistaken is probably the only rock drummer to have penned a spoken poem on a number one hit, namely Nights in White Satin. His work as a rock drummer spans a career of over forty years and, along with his band, has created a musical legacy that began as part of the historic British invasion of the USA by UK musicians during the 1960s. Graeme's lyrics have ignited the passions and hearts of literally millions of music lovers over the decades, and in doing so have attained a legendary status within the music business.

To this day he still tours the world, invoking an almost adolescent response to his appearance on stage. As I'm lucky enough to experience working alongside Graeme as a backing musician, I can affirm his creativity burns as brightly today as it has ever done.

So without further ado, I give you the poetry of Graeme Edge.

Gordon Marshall

Days of Future Passed

*N*ot many people know this, but Morning Glory refers to an hallucinogenic drug, the plant Convolvulus – common name Morning Glory. It produces seeds which, when chewed, produce the desired hallucinogenic effect.

During the making of the album Days of Future Passed, we were, in fact, still doing gigs in the evening, which meant us driving to various points of the compass to get to the different gigs. At the time our only transport was a small Morris 1100 which seated four, and a blue Volkswagen van (for the equipment), which seated two.

We were into the swing of recording after each gig, well into the early hours of the morning, then rushing the tape to Peter Knight who would write a musical bridge to connect our various individual songs to make one continuous piece. The idea of the album was the story of a day in the life of one man – i.e. Days of Future Passed.

This plan had one glaring weakness in that being musicians, all five members of The Moody Blues had very little experience of life between dawn and noon. As such we were short of an opening for the album, moving us from night to through to the gloaming of dawn.

> **I had the pleasure, even though accidental, of writing the bookends for our most successful album!**

    So on this particular day it was my turn to sit in the Volkswagen van, and being aware of the lack of material, I split open a packet of Player's Navy Cut 64 cigarettes to use as parchment – my plan being to write the lyrics for a song moving from night to daylight and back to night.

That evening in the studio, I presented this questionable work of art to the rest of the boys, whose comments were (although they enjoyed it) basically that it was way too wordy to be sung. Whereupon Tony Clarke our producer intoned that he thought it was a fine poem, and that it would sit nicely on a piece of music written by Peter Knight representing both the beginning and the end of a single day. And thus I had the pleasure, even though accidental, of writing the bookends for our most successful album, Days of Future Passed.

The Day Begins

Morning Glory

Cold-hearted orb that rules the night
Removes the colours from our sight
Red is grey, and yellow, white
But we decide which is right
And which is an illusion

Pinprick holes in a colourless sky
Let insipid flickers of light pass by
The mighty light of ten thousand suns
Challenges infinity and is soon gone
Night time, to some a brief interlude
To others the fear of solitude

Brave Helios, wake up your steeds
Bring the warmth the countryside needs

Late Lament

Breathe deep the gathering gloom,
Watch lights fade from every room
Bedsitter people look back and lament
Another day's useless energy spent

Impassioned lovers wrestle as one
Lonely man cries for love and has none
New mother picks up and suckles her son
Senior citizens wish they were young

Cold-hearted orb that rules the night
Removes the colours from our sight
Red is grey and yellow, white
But we decide which is right
And which is an illusion

In Search of The Lost Chord

Departure

Be it sight, sound, smell or touch
There's something inside that we need so much

The sight of a touch, or the scent of a sound
Or the strength of an oak with roots, deep in the ground
The wonder of flowers, to be covered, and then to burst up
Through tarmac, to the sun again, or to fly to the sun
Without burning a wing, to lie in a meadow
And hear the grass sing

To have all these things
In our memories hoard, and to use them
To help us, to find the lost chord

The Word

This garden universe vibrates complete
Some, we get a sound so sweet

Vibrations, reach on up to become light
And then through gamma, out of sight

Between the eyes and ears there lie
The sounds of colour and the light of a sigh

And to hear the sun, what a thing to believe
But it's all around if we could but perceive

To know ultra-violet, infra-red, and x-rays
Beauty to find in so many ways

Two notes of the chord, that's our poor scope
And to reach the chord is our life's hope

And to name the chord is important to some
So they give it a word, and the word is OM

On the Threshold of a Dream

The inspiration for this came from an experience on our first trip to America. Although we had been to America before – we had played in New York – we'd never actually been on the road in America. On this one particular occasion we had been in Chicago, and we had to head back to New York, but we had no idea how far it was – it looked about four and half inches on the map, but of course a scaled map of America is somewhat different from one of England.

We headed out in what I think was a Chevrolet Impala, but none of us had driven an automatic car before. So when we finally got it going forward, unbeknownst to us, we got it stuck in the second of three gears. We hammered it all the way from Chicago to New York in second. We knew American cars were gas-guzzlers, so that didn't give it away; we just thought it wasn't very fast. We were pushing it up to 75mph, poor little thing; they had to put a new engine in it when we took it back.

Part of that experience included going from a green and leafy Chicago, and as we headed to New York, gradually driving into autumn. The first thing I noticed was the odd tree moving into autumn shades. Then I noticed they looked like British silver birch – in fact they're called white birch, a very similar tree, but the colours are very much more powerful. The reds are actually scarlet, the yellows a brilliant canary yellow, not the sort of reddish brown and murky beige that we get in England.

> **It was the old circle of life theme that a thousand people have written about, but this was my attempt at it.**

It's called the crimson tide. I remember we were spotting trees here and there, and we came into one valley where one side was still green, with one or two scattered colours, and the other side of the valley had turned to autumn. It looked absolutely beautiful and stunning. Also as we continued, we lost autumn and came to bare trees, which gave me – in one drive – a real perspective on the cycle of life. Going from green trees to bare trees put my mind in the position of storing the information to write something about.

That became "the white eagle of the North", which is of course the snow clouds, followed by the "browns, reds and golds of autumn, lie in the gutter, dead". And "summer hope" is the cycle of the leaves, fertilising the ground, so that animals can grow from it. It was the old circle of life theme that a thousand people have written about, but this was my attempt at it.

The Dream

When the white eagle of the North
Is flying overhead
And the browns, reds and golds of autumn
Lie in the gutter, dead

Remember then, the summer birds
With wings of fire flaying
Come to witness spring's new hope
Born of leaves decaying

As new life will come from death
Love will come at leisure
Love of love, love of life
And giving without measure

Gives in return a wondrous yearn
Of a promise almost seen
Live hand-in-hand
And together we'll stand

On the threshold of a dream...

In the Beginning

First Man:
I think...
I think I am.
Therefore I am!
I think...

Establishment:
Of course you are, my bright little star...
I've miles and miles of files
Pretty files of your forefather's fruit
And now to suit our great computer
You're magnetic ink!

First Man:
I'm more than that
I know I am...
At least, I think I must be

Inner Man:
There you go, man
Keep as cool as you can
Face piles of trials with smiles
It riles them to believe
That you perceive
The web they weave...
And keep on thinking free

4

To our Children's Children's Children

This was on the album To Our Children's Children's Children. I think with the exception of Days of Future Passed, this was the album that had been thematically the most developed and clearest in our brains before we started it, and was very much the brainchild of Tony Clarke. It was at the time of the famous space race, when we saw the moon landings (which affected us all), and films such as 2001: A Space Odyssey, which were released around the same time... it was all getting a bit grandiose.

And while it was a magnificent achievement, it suddenly struck me that we actually, literally in terms of space travel, had only gone to the next county... we'd only just gone down the road. It was 250,000 miles, and in the scheme of things, that's nothing.

So I attempted to juxtapose the two things: "Blasting, billowing, bursting forth with the power of ten billion" offered the magnificence or hugeness of the achievement, and then ending it with "butterfly sneezes" was me trying to counterbalance that with the feeling that "We ain't seen nothing yet." And it sort of carried on from there.

I was inspired by that famous shot where the astronauts are standing on the moon looking back at the globe, which creates the reaction of, "Whoa... that's all of us... ALL of us... over there." This led to the line "Conceiving the heavens clear of misty shroud", which suggests getting the scales off your eyes, and realising it's one planet, one people and only one hope... us.

> 66 I was inspired by that famous shot where the astronauts are standing on the moon looking back at the globe. 99

Higher and Higher

Blasting, billowing, bursting forth
With the power of ten billion butterfly sneezes
Man, with his flaming pyre
Has conquered the wayward breezes

Climbing to tranquillity
Far above the cloud
Conceiving the heavens
Clear of misty shroud
Higher and higher
Now we've learned to play with fire
Go higher
And higher
And higher
Vast vision must improve our sight
Perhaps at last we'll see an end
To our homes endless blight
And the beginning of the Free

Climb to tranquillity
Finding its real worth
Conceiving the heavens
Flourishing on earth
Higher and higher
Now we've learned to play with fire
We go higher
And higher
And higher

5

Question of Balance

This track, or poem... or prose, to give it a more accurate name, started as a song – a light-hearted ballad, really – by Ray Thomas and was typical of Ray's more whimsical side. I believe some over-medication went on in the studio, because the thing just took off and got grander and grander and more musically overdubbed and stretched, and everybody just got carried away.

Carried away, that is, until it was time for Ray to put the lyric on and it just didn't fit – we had managed to totally massacre his song, changing it into something that was no longer viable as his song, or at least what he had intended it to be. We were all sitting around wondering what to do, with everyone throwing in ideas. I remember it well: I was sitting in the control room soaking up the atmosphere like a sponge, and I found I had a feeling for what everyone was saying – especially a couple of things that Tony Clarke said, which really got into me. So, I turned to everyone and said, "Give me 15 minutes, and I'll come back with an idea." What I was going to do was just write down an idea and ask for a couple of days to turn it into something that we could use as a lyric.

> ❝ As it is a little biblical, maybe this was the start of what became known as our pretentious period! ❞

I didn't bother about trying to make anything rhyme, I just wrote down the ideas as they came to me... a stream of consciousness. I quickly went back into the studio and read it to them. At first the control room was totally silent, and I thought I'd blown it. Tony Clarke was the first to speak and he said, "I feel humbled," which was rather a shock, as I wasn't expecting that. Everyone else said they thought it was fantastic, so we got Mike Pinder to put his whisky-and-cigarettes baritone voice to it, to give it some timbre, and we put it on the record.

The Balance

After he had journeyed
And his feet were sore
And he was tired
He came upon an orange grove
And he rested

And he lay in the cool
And while he rested
He took to himself an orange
And tasted it
And it was good

And he felt the earth to his spine
And he asked
And he saw the tree above him
And the stars
And the veins in the leaf
And the light
And the balance

And he saw magnificent perfection
Whereon, he thought of himself in balance
And he knew he was

Just open your eyes
And realise
The way it's always been
Just open your mind
And you will find
The way it's always been
Just open your heart
And that's a start

And he thought of those he angered
For he was not a violent man
And he thought of those he hurt
For he was not a cruel man

And he thought of those he frightened
For he was not an evil man
And he understood…
He understood himself

Upon this he saw
That when he was full of anger
Or knew hurt
Or felt fear
It was because he was not understanding

And he learned
~~Compassion~~

And with his eye of compassion
He saw his enemies like unto himself

And he learned
~~Love~~

Then, he was answered

Just open your eyes
And realise
The way it's always been
Just open your mind
And you will find
The way it's always been
Just open your heart
And that's a start

↔

> **The thing that was mostly on my mind...
> was the American President at the time.**

*O*bviously when working closely together, there is a hell of a lot of cross-pollination that goes on in the studio. Pindi (Mike Pinder) had written a song called, How Is It (We Are Here) on the A Question of Balance album, and he was a verse short. On many occasions with my poems, people would pull together and put music behind it. Obviously with the couple or three songs I've written (like 22,000 Days for instance), the guys gave me an awful lot of music, so I was perfectly happy to give Pindi a hand with the lyrics on this particular song.

The thing that was mostly on my mind and was concerning me a great deal was the American president at the time – I believe it was Jimmy Carter – who had decided to stop sending grain to the Russians as part of an attempt to pressurise them into some political move or another. And I personally found that very scary, because I really like the doctrine of MAD (Mutually Assured Destruction), as I didn't think anyone was going to start World War Three knowing that we would all die in a nuclear holocaust... the difference being if a man is sitting in a tank and his kids have got no bread, he will come to fetch bread.

So I was very upset by the fact that a) we were not giving bread to the Russians, and b) we were openly pouring it into the sea, throwing it away instead of giving to them, which I thought was unnecessarily aggressive.

> Men's mighty mine-machines
> Digging in the ground
> Stealing rare minerals
> Where they can be found
> Concrete caves with iron doors
> Bury it again
> While a starving, frightened world
> Fills the sea with grain

Don't You Feel Small

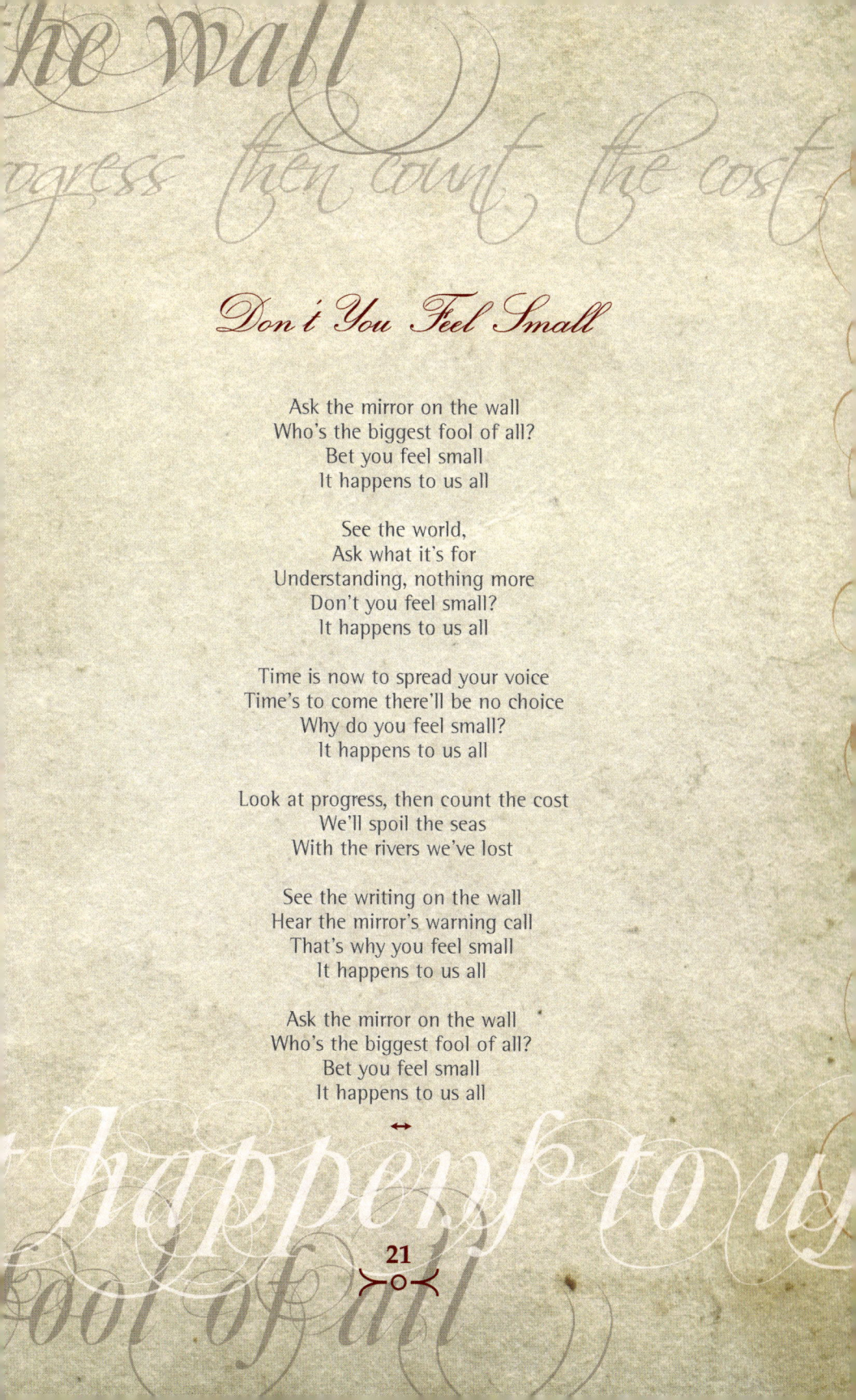

Ask the mirror on the wall
Who's the biggest fool of all?
Bet you feel small
It happens to us all

See the world,
Ask what it's for
Understanding, nothing more
Don't you feel small?
It happens to us all

Time is now to spread your voice
Time's to come there'll be no choice
Why do you feel small?
It happens to us all

Look at progress, then count the cost
We'll spoil the seas
With the rivers we've lost

See the writing on the wall
Hear the mirror's warning call
That's why you feel small
It happens to us all

Ask the mirror on the wall
Who's the biggest fool of all?
Bet you feel small
It happens to us all

Every Good Boy Deserves Favour

After You Came

Since it began I got one dream
And really it's my only blessing
If I can come through then so can you
And you will find there's no regretting
Things you want from your life's font
Will never let your spirit roam
Come back to earth for what it's worth
For you've been dreaming of a ceiling not a home

I've been doing my best
What else can I do?
Is there something I've missed
That will help you through?

I have reached the top of my wall
And all I've found is another way to fall

For some short time
For a while you and I were joined to eternity
Then we split in two, back to me and you
Like the rain rising from the sea
Rising from the sea
We all can see what we shall be
But knowing's really not controlling

With time perhaps I will pass the traps
And find some peace and understanding
After you'd come and while you're gone
You leave me guessing – it's depressing

Never to know the way to go
To find some time along a little less pressing
So you just have to laugh
When it hurts so much
You're so far away and so hard to touch

I have reached the top of my wall
And all I've found is another way to fall

7

Seventh Sojourn

This was one of those writing occasions - a little like the one I alluded to with Mike Pinder - where an enormous amount of cross-pollination went on and everybody gave and received freely from everybody else. The only consideration for everybody involved was to satisfactorily complete the album.

With one particular song Justin had all the music written, including the melody; he also had lyrics for one verse and the chorus. I would say he had basically seven-eighths of the song completed. All he needed help with was just one verse, so I gladly pitched in. As it was so long ago, I can't really remember, but we were probably working on it together when we wrote the verses *"There's a leafless tree in Asia"* and *"the pain of a burning wound"* (the latter of which sounds much more like me than Justin), and I thought that was the end of it.

Justin had written music for a couple of my things and just left it at that, so I was just happy to be able to help Justin with this song, which was reward enough. However, in an act of extraordinary generosity - totally unexpected and, I would say, undeserved - he gave me half of the publishing. This means it's as if I had written all of the lyrics for the song, as opposed to just one verse. In terms of the lyrics I had written less than 20%, but that was the way things were in those days. I will always remember that gratefully.

> **❝** I was just happy to be able to help Justin with this song, which was reward enough. However... **❞**

You and Me

There's a leafless tree in Asia
Under the sun there's a homeless man
There's a forest fire in the valley
Where the story all began

What will be our last thought?
Do you think it's coming soon?
Will it be a comfort
Or the pain of a burning wound?

All we are trying to say
Is we are all we've got
You and me just cannot fail
If we never, never stop

You're an ocean full of faces
And you know that we believe
We're just a wave that drifts around you
Singing all our hopes and dreams

We look around in wonder
At the work that has been done
By the visions of our father
Touched by his loving son

All we are trying to say
Is we are all we've got
You and me just cannot fail
If we never, never stop

All we are trying to say
Is we are all we've got
You and me just cannot fail
If we never, never stop

You and me just cannot fail
If we never, ever, never, ever stop

8

Octave

*I*n 1977 we were chased out of the country by Harold Wilson's government, which, if I remember correctly, charged us 83% tax, which in turn forced upon me the incredible hardship of having to go and live in the South of France – something I had to learn to live with. Strangely enough, I rented a villa (as it's called), which happened to be next door to the one owned by no less a luminary than Brigitte Bardot. I promise you that in the three months I was there prior to moving to America, she never took up residence once. And I knew this because I could see her swimming pool by hanging from the left-hand chimney pot of my roof by a seven-foot-long rope.

Over the course of that time, I was with my second wife, who was nursing my brand-new son Matthew who was born at the end of October of that year. This was April, so he was about five or six months old during the stay there. During that time I became enamoured with the little chap, and this is one of those songs that when you sit down to write it runs out of you like... well, you don't feel like you're writing it yourself, it feels more like you're a conduit, as it just comes out: no corrections, no changes, every line rhymes, every metre is fine, it just runs straight through you like a lightning bolt. The whole thing was written in less than twenty minutes, including the melody (well, what melody there is), which was also in my mind. Of course once we were in the studio the guys very nicely rallied round, and made a song out of my little hodgepodge of bits and dabs, for which I'll be eternally grateful.

Life is here

❝ The whole thing was written in twenty minutes, including the melody ❞

I'll be Level with You

Little guy
Little hands
Little eyes
And lots of time.
What are you going to be?
What you going to see
When your eyes are level with mine?

I'll be level with you
I don't know what I would do
If I had to face the things
That you've got coming down the line

Lots of luck
Lots of health
Lots of wealth
And little pain
That's what I want for you
But there's little I can do
To put you on the gravy train

I'll be level with you
You'll always end up coming through
But you'll find yourself
Lost in space now and again

Life is here

But you have to have a world you can live in
Not a world where all the hope is gone
And as long as we are here together
We'll try to build a home for the free

Filled with pity not pain
That's loving and sane
Not divided by hate
And living in spite
Until it's too late

Life is here
Love will come
In the end;
Give it time
There's wonders still to do
And I know you'll find it's true
That yours will be bigger than mine

I'll be level with you
The one thing I hope you will do
Is tell me about what you're doing
From time to time.

Tell me about what you're doing
From time to time

9

Long Distance Voyager

22,000 Days

Even though I know it's only me
And my dreams
That drive me so
Let me go, please
Let me go onto tomorrow
One day at a time
Now I know the only foe is time

22,000 days
22,000 days
It's not a lot
It's all you've got
22,000 days

22,000 nights
22,000 nights
It's all you know
So start the show and this time
This time, feel the flow
And get it right!

Now the time when I first saw you
Is over and gone
Then I knew my life with you would go on
Knowing you so much longer
I've a changing mind
Change for you
You have changed to mine

Time's the only real wealth

22,000 days
22,000 days
It's not a lot
It's all you've got
22,000 days

22,000 nights
22,000 nights
It's all you know
So start the show and this time
This time, feel the flow
And get it right!

Everybody knows
It always shows
Wasting time's an aggravation
No time for confrontation
You want to take a lot
By love, by law or stealth
Time's the only real wealth
You have got

Even though I know it's only me
And my dreams
That drive me so
Let me go, please
Let me go into tomorrow
One day at a time
Now I know the only foe is time

22,000 days
I've got 22,000 days
It's not a lot
It's all you've got
22,000 days

We've got 22,000 nights
22,000 nights
It's all you know
So start the show
22,000 days

22,000 days
22,000 days
It's not a lot
It's all you got
22,000 days

22,000 nights
22,000 nights
It's all you know
So start the show
22,000 ways

Time's the only real wealth

Graeme Edge on tour with the Moody blues in the USA
March 2012

10

The Present

Going Nowhere

Once more I've loved I've laughed and I've lost
Now I'm alone left counting the cost
Once more sweet child of middling years
Basted again in bitter-sweet tears
I will survive solitude
But come alive
I'll love anew

Somebody tell me you love me
Somebody tell me you care
I've got a heart full of giving
Going nowhere (going nowhere)

Daylight will come and steal the night sights
Starlight on black replaced with grey light
Now I must go out and set my best pace
Running all day in the human race
But now I know the good news
Before you win you have to lose

Somebody tell me you love me (somebody tell me)
Somebody tell me you care (tell me you care)
I've got a heart full of giving
Going nowhere (going nowhere)

How much longer must I travel on
Looking for someone to help me (help me) sing my song?
How much longer will it be?
I need to find someone
For the love (find someone for the life, of me)
From me

Somebody tell me you love me (somebody tell me)
Somebody tell me you care (tell me you care)
I've got a heart full of giving
Going nowhere (going nowhere)

11

The Other Side of Life

This was from the album we made in 1986. Here I was experimenting with the title The Other Side of Life – what is life, what are the major forces of life? The usual pragmatic topics such as economics really didn't hold any answers for me, as there really is only one powerful source and that is Love. And there really is only one wealth and that is Time. I was trying to put that together in a way to make people, including myself, maybe value those two things a little bit more than a new Jag.

> ❝ ...there is only one powerful source and that is Love. ❞

The Spirit

The sun and moon every day
Day and night mark my play

See the future in the past
Try to change or make it last

Go for broke – don't regret
Get your hands dirty get your feet wet

Take your place – use me well
I'm in your hands so make me tell

A broken dream seems unkind
But I can help for I am time

I can heal you – it's not a matter of slight
Only of sound let me feel for you
Feel for yourself the love all around
I can lead you; is your soul afraid
Of what you've made?

Do you know the way the spirit goes
All around on the wind?
Distant whispers of what I bring
In the day in the night
Locked in words of lovers' delight

If I'm lost or mislaid
Just keep looking, don't be afraid
In the eye on the mind
I'm everywhere and yours to find
I'm not far just discover
I'm in you for I am love

Strange Times

Nothing Changes

The dark cloak of winter's war
Left a future still unsure
Sitting in a class
Of the future's past
We saw a list of dates
And we knew we would last
To see them all
1984 was a year to fear
Hope was dead, a police state here
Halley's Comet was to fly by
And we would see a shining in the night sky
Now 2001 is soon to come
And just as soon will have come and gone
Nothing changes

Standing at the crossroads
Of what is, will be, and was
The obvious eludes us
Not because the zeroes line up
We should change our way of thought
More if we do not, the way ahead
Is dangerously fraught
And if we did the things we all know to be right
Left would be the childish fears
Of danger in the night
We, each of us are fine
For we have all heard the word
But grouped together
Babel's triumph stampedes
The thoughtless herd
Nothing changes
Nothing changes
And nothing stays the same
And life is still
A simple game

13

Kick off Your Muddy Boots

With this song I was thinking (and I don't know if you would call it two things, or one thing with two different aspects), but I started off by thinking about the pure physical body that we're in, what it's made up of at the atomic level; not the blood, bone and sinew level, but the cellular and atomic level, where the minerals that we all require – sodium, iron, copper, zinc, all the things that would render us non-viable if we didn't have them in us – take up residence.

The only place those minerals can be formed is in the heart of an exploding star; it's the only place where the pressures are significant enough that the extra electrons and such can be forced into the atom. As that star explodes, it's scattered all over everywhere, and somehow or other, all those various pieces coalesce into a cloud of hot dust at first, then down into a sun and planets, then those bits of dust that are now you and me happen to form into a planet, in what they call a goldilocks zone: not too hot, not too cold, where life as we understand it can exist.

And then life starts: a little amoeba, and we all know the story of that. Following that, somehow or other from a long line of winners, through all the disasters, all the floods, all the comet hits, the meteorite hits, the dinosaurs eating you for breakfast, all the terrible things, plagues, wars, we're now sitting here as survivors, winners. It's quite remarkable. Winning the lottery is nothing compared with the odds of us being alive with me writing this and you reading it.

without command

> ❝ ...I started off by thinking about the pure physical body that we're in, what it's made up of at the atomic level; ❞

Other parts of the song deal more with the cellular level. For instance, the line *"I'm still the same, though the meat has all changed".* As we all know we're sloughing off old cells and growing new cells all the time, replacing bone and sinew, and I think the eye gets changed every 48 hours. The fact of the matter is, it's generally accepted we totally change everything every seven years. And yet you're still you, you still have your memories, you still have the essence of you, which for me is sort of proof of the spirituality (call it soul, call it chi, call it whatever you want) of the human and probably all life.

That's the background to this piece of literary, er, nonsense.

Lost in Space

I'm just in space like the rest of my race,
Changing cells from the day I was born.
But I'm still the same, though the meat has all changed,
Something's holding me together that's for sure

I find myself suspended in a vacuum
A vacuum that goes either way
But there must be something else to it
Because the sun comes to me every day

When I see the truth I see it with my own imagery
It's my brain lying, trying to make me see
That the truth is so big that it runs eternity
And small enough to fit inside me

Far away past a star into the void inside of me
Or smaller past the atoms that have nothing inside
Just the same as a car or a leaf or a star
Cannot move without command
Something moves me and without it I'd be no more living
Than a hole in the sand

Hold my hand, feel its warm touch from the fire inside
Hold my heart, feel its beating, how I can't decide
I don't control my sleeping or when I dream away
But there must be something to it
For I wake up every day

Shoigun

Far off in a distant land
A man lying dead in the sand
Lying by his side was a song
Written down on a parchment fair

Overgrown with ageing hair
You could see this man died alone

From riding shotgun on the 4.42

Riding shotgun was his dream
But he's fallen dead it seems

Riding shotgun on the 4.42

When the sun it got too hot
I was glad of what I'd got
Living on the food that I found
Twenty minutes left to go

Another town's in sight you know
Think I'll rest my boots while I can

Riding shotgun on the 4.42

Here comes Lucy Springer
You know that she's a ringer
She'll take you for a ride for a while
You know that she looks fancy

Much more slick than Nancy
You know you'll have to pay for a smile

Riding shotgun on the 4.42

I know that I haven't been mean
And I always kept my sixguns clean
And I feel I'm at the end of my road
I'll make way for someone new

Do you think it could be you
As I lie face down dead in the road?

Riding shotgun on the 4.42

Something We'd Like to Say

There's something we'd like to say
About the way that we feel today
You know we'd just like to float away
In the end it must be that way

You know that nothing is real or true
Unless it happened to me or you
And you just have to come on through
You know there's nothing else you can do

Last night I nearly died,
I nearly cried
My heart inside me aches me
Takes me
Breaks me
Fakes me so
No sign of love no hope of anything

In Dreams

In dreams you know I'm learning
All the time I keep turning
Trying to be the one

But you know I wish I could show you
Just what is inside my head
That makes me feel
The way I do

In dreams sometimes I'm aching
Hoping for someone to wake me
Running for my life
Running for my life
All night

But you know how hard it can be
Living like a dreamer like me
Sometimes afraid oh! So afraid
In my dreams

Have You Ever Wondered

Have you ever wondered what you would do
If the world was sweet and
Kind exactly like you?
Would you be afraid?
Of what you got
Would you try to own a tree?
Well you cannot

Tell me the fruit is yours grown off a tree?
Tell me you grew and don't you see
You didn't grow it, you're not
The sun or the rain?
And if you went away it would grow again

Sometimes I wonder
What it is I see
Is it the world around us?
Or is it me?

Il lie awake wondering what went wrong
The world was ours for a song

14

Paradise Ballroom

This interview covers the entire Paradise Ballroom album.

This was the second of my solo albums. By this point I'd learned quite a bit and acquired much more knowledge about the whole recording process, and had gained confidence in getting things a little more the way I wanted them and become better at expressing myself. I had more command of the engineering process and got things done my way. As it developed – about half-way through – I suddenly realised that what I was doing was trying to take this hooligan threesome and make a Moody Blues album. I suddenly thought, I'll finish this album but then it's time to stop messing about and get back with my friends and start making proper music.

Paradise Ballroom

You've got to save your city
Don't let it fall
Don't let it change your life
Because it's a pity if you're letting someone come and steal your wife
And he thinks she's still pretty

Save your city
Fight for your belief
Don't let them change your side
Or pay you off with money, honey
I'm not fooling, I'm going to change my city

> "...I'll finish this album but then it's time to stop messing around and get back with my friends and start making proper music."

Two-time losers, save yourselves,
The fourth time's going to give you up, if you let it.
I just tell it, tell it on passing by.
Can you tell me the way to the terrible city in the sky?
To Paradise Ballroom?

Fallen city from a rock to a pebble
That's how you smash my frills
Not a bird, there's nowhere to land, it has to take to the hills
You've had your cake and you'd better eat it

Fallen lovers,
So sad to see you gamble with your lives
You've had your bellies filled with card games and all those fights
It's about time you chose right

Don't you know you've got to save your city?
Don't let it fall
Don't let it change your life
Because it's a pity if you're letting someone come and steal your wife
And you think she's still pretty

Paradise Ballroom, where are you today?
The tension of my evenings
I thought they were great
So pray for the people
I still get off for free
At the Paradise Ballroom, my friends and me

Human

I want to be the one,
Don't want to be the two.
I want to be the lover,
Don't want be a fool.

I'm not going to be your stepping-stone
You can't walk on me,
Because I'm only human
Because I'm only human, you see.

Don't laugh about my face
Because I found mine in space
And you found yours in a fancy-dress parade
Oh what a move, smooth as cream
She's nothing like I've ever seen
But she's only human
Yes, she's only human
You know, she's only human, to me

Some say she's as cold as ice
Better leave her, get smart and get wise
But I cannot hear their cries
Humiliation I can stand
When only I take her by the hand
Because she's only human
Because she's only human, to me

↔

Down, Down, Down

Down, down, down is the mood I'm in
Since you've been away
Lost in the world, my stomach's sick with pain
I can't stand the day.

To be in love
It's just a phase I'm going through
Because I still love you.
You tore me down so bad
To your friends, I know
You forgot the good times, girl
The time will show

To be apart
It's just a phase we're going through
Because I still love you

You say you want to leave, run with the wind
Moving on, baby, is no sin
But what about the love you had for me?
It just can't fade away

To stay in one place
And watch something grow
Is a feeling you're never going to know
If you stay away from me
Don't stay away from me

Don't stay away from me
When I see you walking by
The shadows in your eyes just say it all

Down, down, down is the mood I'm in
Since you've been away
Lost in the world, my stomach's sick with pain
I can't stand the day

To be in love
It's just a phase I'm going through,
Because I still love you

In The Night Of The Light

Take a look at my face,
You've seen it so many times
Across the Chicago state line
Reflected in a bottle of wine

I'm taking a chance on the night,
Restless moon's a-dancing in the sky
And the beauty's running through my eyes
In the light of the night

You're as young as the hills
Timeless rivers running through your eyes
And your beauty is ok no disguise
In the light of the night

I took a look at your face
I've seen it so many times
Across the Chicago state line
Reflected in a bottle of wine

Take a look at my face
You've seen it so many times
Across the Chicago state line
Reflected in a bottle of wine

I'm taking a chance on the night
Restless moon's a-dancing in the sky
And the beauty's running through my eyes
In the night of the light

Be My Eyes

Travelling along on a beam of light
Looking for friends who will be on my side and tell me no lies
Travelling along holding hands with faith
Searching out places darker than night skies
And deeper than love lie

So hard to see
Will you be my eyes?

Travelling along with a dream of a voyage
I'm hoping to find a lost city and new world that I must see
Look here, my friend, see me tremble with fear
I've lost all companions, stay close as we coast
Through a lifetime of journeys, an endless sea
My companion, the voyage, and me

Be my eyes

Travelling along on a beam of light
Looking for friends who will be on my side and tell me no lies
Travelling along holding hands with faith
Searching out places darker than night skies
And-a deeper than love lies

So hard to see
Will you be my eyes?

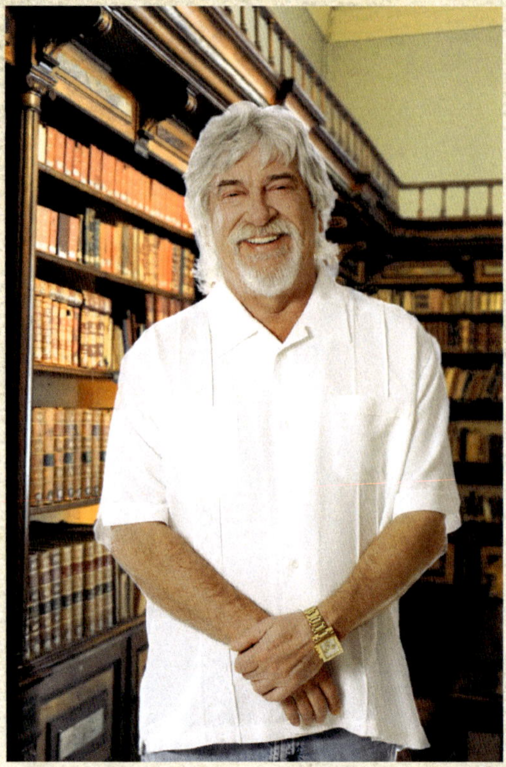

Made in United States
Orlando, FL
15 December 2021